SAP APO Interview Questions, Answers, and Explanations:
SAP APO Certification Review

By: Jens Schmeer

SAP APO Interview Questions, Answers, and Explanations: SAP APO Certification Review

ISBN-13 978-1933804-42-4

Edited By: Jamie Fisher

Preface

This book is intended to be a compendium of example situations and problems for beginners as well as more advanced users to have a starting point troubleshooting, to gain deeper understanding or to have a check list of possible solutions they maybe haven't considered yet.

Taking questions out of the overall context can be problematic since it doesn't draw the complete picture of a situation or a problem as they might occur or have occurred.

Often times the consultants on-site on a project and have a more detailed understanding of a situation. Consequently it is hardly possible to answer this question or give recommendations considering every possibility.

With the answers provided in this book to such questions, as they might occur in projects, it is not intended to undermine your on-site consultants and expert's credibility. They might work towards a specific roadmap or solution and had to rule out certain options that are offered in this book.

Please keep this "bigger picture" in mind when applying, testing and researching the provided solutions. After all, your problem might be unique and could require opening a customer message to SAP to get resolved.

Table of contents

Demand Planning (DP)

Question 1: Data load errors

"I am getting the following errors in the data loads In APO Quality system during monitoring checks: This is a quality client copied system from the APO production system.

1. There is no PSA for info source LISVCIT and source system AP900.
2. System error occurred (RFC call).
3. Activation of data records is terminated.

How do I fix these errors?"

A. You actually describe 3 different problems. To solve the first error, check that the InfoPackage is not loading directly into the InfoCube. Make sure that it is loading to PSA first before going into the cube.

With errors 2 and 3, there seems to be a problem with whichever system is calling your client, and you should talk to your basis team to rectify RFC errors. If all efforts don't lead to the desired results you probably will have to open an OSS message to SAP.

Question 2: Sales History for DP

"We are trying to remove the duplicate storage of sales history data in two places and the consequent system overheads of loads and other similar items. Is it always necessary to load sales history into APO or can it be stored in the central BW (non-APO) and referenced via a remote cube in APO?"

A. Having the Sales History stored in APO does not necessarily mean that you have duplicate data. The central BW (non –APO) is the leading system where the Sales History is stored. The only reason why it is "stored" in the APO-BW is to load it into liveCache.
Typically Sales History in APO is updated at the beginning of each planning cycle (e.g. over the weekend) and the previous weeks one is deleted.

If you want to avoiding having Sales Order History data stored in an InfoCube in APO you can use a remote cube in the APO BW. For example the Sales Order History Cube is maintained in the main BW System and a remote cube is created in the APO BW system based on the Sales Order History cube in the main BW system.

Question 3: No Entry for BW_USER in the table RSADMIN

"I am maintaining a source system in the Administration workbench of the APO by the Menu Supply chain planning-Demand Planning-Basic setting-Administrator workbench. Once I create source system type Sap-r/3 Manual creation selection and selected the R/3 Destination and logical system name from the Popup menu, the system indicates 'No entry for BW_USER in the table RSADMIN is available'.

When I check for details, the following information is given:
'No entry for BW_USER in table RSADMIN available;
Message no. RSAR 059
Diagnosis: Missing entry in table RSADMIN
System Response: Process for creating a source system terminated.'

I then went to the table RSADMIN. It is having entry for BW_USER as

'Object BW_USER' and further indicated: 'Value ALLREMOTE'

When I need to maintain another entry in this table, I plan to load the data from Sap/r3 Info structure to APO Info cube. For this I am going to do the following setting:
Procedure: In Customizing> maintain Proposal for Users in the Source System: BW Customizing Implementation Guide -> Business Information Warehouse -> Connections to Other Systems -> Connection between SAP Systems and BW -> Maintain Proposal for Users in the Source System (ALE Communication).

I am concerned though that I might encounter the same response from the system. How do I resolve this issue?"

A. In a situation like this, you should check for the following:

1. Verify if you have the BW_USER set up for both, the R/3 system and the APO system. They need to have the same password set for both systems.
2. Double check if you do not have BWREMOTE user. If you don't have it, go create a remote user (in IMG) and that will fix the problem. Depending on your authorization set-up, this task might have to be performed by your Basis or Administration team.

Question 4: Loading text and master data

"I have encountered some difficulties regarding uploading text and master data in BW Info Object. We want to create our own report on the BW embedded on APO (3.0).

For example, 9ALOCNO has the code but contains no description nor attributes. What kind of activity is necessary for it to work in APO? Do I have to create a custom data source reading /SAPAPO/* tables?"

A. No, you should not have to create a custom data source to read the /SAPAO/* tables. You should be able to load text since 9ALOCNO has a text table and in Interactive Demand Planning you then would be able to see both, the code and the text.
If you are using the standard SAP APO object 9ALOCNO, however, then you will indeed have no attributes since this InfoObject doesn't have attributes defined and hence you can't load any attributes (codes or texts). What you could do, however, create a new InfoObject, i.e. ZALOCNO, as a copy from 9ALOCNO and add the attributes you need for you planning scenario.

Question 5: User Exit for /SAPAPO/TS_PLOBS_GENERATE

"In order to create Character Combinations (CC) in the background, it is possible to use the standard report "/SAPAPO/TS_PLOBS_GENERATE" on the basis of an info cube.

The report also offers obviously the possibility to use a user exit. However, I can't find the right user-exit. Where can I find the right user exit?"

A. Use the BADI: /SAPAPO/SDP_MASTER exit for your purpose. This should solve your problem.

Question 6: Creating a new key figure for a planning book

"I started adding a new key figure in the planning book in DP by using BW admin (rsa1) but it doesn't show in the interactive demand planning book. How do I create or add a new key figure in a planning book in DP?

I did try to go in /sapapo/msdp_admin and select my planning area to add new key figures in there but the system said that there are some active versions and that I can only go in display mode. How can I go in change mode?"

A. If the 2 functionalities ("Administrator Workbench" and "Administration of Supply and Demand Planning") required to create a key figure for a planning book are mixed like in this question you should watch out. It might either be because the questioner doesn't have a strong APO Demand Planning knowledge or it is intended to be a trick question!

There are 2 possible solutions, depending on the purpose of the key figure. If the new key figure is only needed to show the result of a macro calculation but there is no need to save the result, you should use the auxiliary key figure within the planning book. No other points to watch out for and no other actions to be taken.

If the new key figure is supposed to hold data (as a result of a macro calculation or a manual input), which needs to be saved, you need to create a new liveCache key figure.
The first step is to create the key figure InfoObject in the Administrator Workbench (RSA1). It is not possible to assign a key figure to a planning book from the Administrator Workbench!

You will have to add the new key figure InfoObject first to the Planning Area before adding it to the Planning Book. To change the Planning Area you use the "Administration of Demand and Supply Planning"

(/sapapo/msdp_admin).

As of SCM 5.0 you are able to add – and even delete – a key figure from the Planning Area without deactivating it as long as the key figure is not in use in a planning book or macro.

In any previous SCM version you will have to work around the fact that you can only chance INACTIVE Planning Areas. To deactivate the Planning Area you will have to delete the time series object, which will cause the loss of ALL planning data. In order to preserve your production planning data you will have to backup it into an InfoCube.

AFTER the data is backed up, you can proceed to deactivate the Planning Area. Right click on the planning area and select "Delete Time Series Objects". After confirming the warning message the icon next to the Planning Area will change from a green circle to a red square. The Planning Area is now inactive and you can add the new key figure InfoObject.

After you have done the required changed to the Planning Area you can initialize a new time series and you can upload your planning data again from the backup InfoCube.

As the last step you enter the design of the planning book and add the new key figure to your planning book and planning view. After activating the changed Planning Book you will see the new key figure in your Planning View.

Ideally this should be done in your DEV environment first and the changed Planning Area and Planning Book should then be transported into QA and Production. PRIOR to transporting you have to backup the planning data to avoid data losses!

Question 7: Characteristic drilldown

"In the data view of the planning book, we have a number of key figures. When I drill down by product, I get the first key figure and the product drilldown. From there, the next key figure appears and the list goes on.

I would like to swap the drilldown between the characteristics and the drilldown.
Is there a way to change the format so that I can drilldown by the product and show all key figures for each product instead?"

A. This is very easy to achieve because all you have to do is change the pivot sorting. You can do this by right clicking on the name field of your planning table and select Pivot sorting.
It might happen that Pivot sorting is grayed out. Then you have to make sure your header row is on and "Details All" is selected for a characteristic, you're for you product. This is required before the system will allow pivot sorting.

In previous APO versions Pivot sorting couldn't be saved and the users had to set up their sorting every time they entered a planning book or loaded data. As of SCM 4.0 Pivot sorting can be saved user specific and as of SCM 4.1 even a Pivot sorting for key figures is possible.

If your business process requires the users to drill down to the "work" level they either can use the interactive drill down functions via the head or the shuffler or you can develop a macro that would bring the user straight to the "right" level. In general you should test the performance of your drill downs.

Question 8: Storage bucket profile

"We are required to carry out Storage Bucket Profile maintenance in Production system as the horizon of storage bucket profile is getting expired (data backup from planning area has already been taken into cubes). Can I transport it to production by defining a new storage bucket profile into the development system? Or do I have to define it in the Production system directly? If I can transport the storage bucket profile, what is the transaction code for that?"

A. It is common practice to activate the "Storage Bucket Profile" several years out prior to a go-Live – exactly to avoid this situation. The activated horizon should give you about 10 years of planning horizon where there wouldn't be a need to carry out a "Storage Bucket Profile" maintenance. When setting up the storage bucket profile keep also your intended planning horizon in mind.

If you have reached now the point in time to carry out a Storage Bucket Profile maintenance, however, it also might be a good moment to analyze a possible upgrade to the latest release.

If a Storage Bucket Profile maintenance can't be avoided, however, you can use the standard transport connection for DP and SNP using the transaction /SAPAPO/TSOBJ. You will also have to transport the planning area from dev to Prod plus all the relevant details like MPOS, Storage buckets, and planning buckets. Planning books will also get transported if you do not remove them manually from the transport request.

If you don't want to transport the new settings to your productions system you also could just change the storage buckets directly in production. Depending on your system set-up you might have to "open" it for this step, which might not be an option.

In general I would suggest being consistent: transport as much as possible and do as little changes in the production system. As of SCM 5.0 you also have several new options when performing transports.

Question 9: Inputting a Macro Note

"How can I enter or attach a note to a macro in APO 4.1 Macro Workbench or MacroBuilder?"

A. A rather simple question which is a little tricky to answer. In the Macro Workbench, select the row with the Planning Book/View that contains the macros for which you want to create notes for so it is highlighted. Now do a right click and select "Display Macros" from the menu.
Now the screen splits and in the bottom half you see your planning book with all the macros in it. Right click on the macro for which you want to attach a note and select "Edit Macro Note". The screen splits into half, this time vertically, and on the right side you have now the chance to enter a note about the macro. Edit your note and don't forget to save before you leave the screen using the button "Close All" ()

Note:
The question is only referring to attaching a note to macro and not to a cell in the planning grid! To add a note to a cell to the planning grid you load the data, right click to the cell you want to add the note and chose "Display Note". On the bottom of the screen a window appears where the user can enter his notes or read other users notes. An icon as well as the cell color (standard setting) will indicate if the cell contains a note.

Question 10: Proportional Factor

"I need to set the proportion factor between a pack size (level higher) and product for the entire forecasting period.

Example: Under pack size PK1 give 100% for product A for months 1, 2 and 3 and 100 % for product B for the remaining months. This will help me so that after every monthly forecasting run, the plan numbers are disaggregated to the correct product (i.e. the active one for that month).

I can make the changes directly to the proportional factor key figure to achieve the above result but the problem is that every month, the proportional factors will be regenerated (i.e. new sales month included) and because of this, the percentage settings will be lost.

Can anyone suggest a clean approach to handle this problem? I need for the end user to maintain this and not the IT maintenance team. If I need to use macros, can you please give details on how it should work (i.e. the logic)?"

A. There are two possible ways to approach this:

1. Create a new key figure that will hold your proportional factors and make your changes in it – or simply just the values that you don't want APODPDANT to overwrite.
Then copy this key figure back into APODPDANT using a copy macro. Every time you regenerate your prop factors, remember to run a background job that will re-copy the manually adjusted proportional factor back into APODPDANT. Don't keep your APODPDANT key figure row open for editing. Keeping only the manual proportional factor key figure open to edit should be enough.

2. Instead of having macros copying values back and forth you also could try to disaggregate APODPDANT as well as the key figures you want to disaggregate based on a manual maintained

"new proportional factor" (NPF) key figure. That way you only use APODPDANT as a reference and copy it to NPF using a macro only when and on whatever you want it. All changes are made in the new proportional factor key figure.

Question 11: Using fact sheet from one product to determine sales of another product

"The sale of some of our products is based on the sale of another product. For example: a sale of product A will lead to 2 sales of product B. So we should not have to forecast product B since it will be derived from product A.

How do I factor this in APO DP so that forecasting should be automatic for product B?"

A. This sounds as if the DP BOM (= Bill of material) functionality would be a perfect fit for this requirement.

With the DP BOM functionality you can forecast dependent requirements. The system determines the component parts of finished products through the production process model (PPM) or the production data structure (PDS).

Question 12: Global view of Demand

We have created demand planning areas for different regions in Europe, Americas, and Asia.

If I want to have a Global view of my demand, what do I need to do?

Is there a similar concept to a BW MultiCube available in APO, kind of a "Multi Planning Area" or something?

A. No, I am afraid not. APO doesn't have a function similar to the concept of a MultiCube in BW. Ideally – and if possible - you should only create one planning area for different regions. Since you have already created a Multiplan, you might want to create another small Planning Area just for the Global Demand view. This Planning Area doesn't need to have many key figures and you should be able to use an aggregated level to view the data. Copy the planning data from the different Planning Areas into the new Planning Area to see your global demands in one view.

If it is not necessary to interactively see or work on the data from different regions in Demand Planning you also can extract the contents of the different region Planning Areas into BW. Here you then have the chance to create a MultiCube on top and obtain the required information via BeX report.

Question 13: Selection ID in macro

"I am in need of a selection ID in macro to send the information or save the information in a z table. The objective for this is to essentially monitor which selection ids are being used and by whom, in the interactive planning. How do I fetch a selection ID in macro?"

A. The solution is simple enough. Use table /SAPAPO/TS_SELKO. Here you find the information necessary to complete your macro.

Question 14: Planning book problems

"I encountered two problems in my planning book design:

1) I want certain key figures to be input/output and others as output only in my data view. When I went into design view of the Planning book and right clicked on the selected key figure and made it as output, all the other key figures were also grayed out. Not trusting the design view, I checked in interactive planning and it is indeed setting all of the key figures to output only. I further checked and found there is no grouping on the key figures.

2) Typically, in interactive planning, those time buckets in the history are grayed out (output only) yet this is not occurring. I have checked my storage bucket profile and periodicities and all seem fine.

As far as I am aware this is not a GUI problem, as I am on a recent GUI patch. How do I resolve these issues?"

A. This sounds familiar and what you describe is probably one of the more common problems that can happen using APO. In general SAP is constantly improving the software and you apply these updated then via the service stacks (know in the past as service packs). As a consequence, sometimes the patch level of your GUI is out of date to display certain information correctly – like in your case described.
You should be able to fix these problems by installing the latest release of the GUI. In some cases there are project guidelines on the roll-out of a new GUI, which you have to follow. I also would highly recommend that you ensure that you have the latest versions of the SCM and BW add-ons (separate files).

Optional as of SCM 5.0 SAP will introduce a new GUI, which should help to reduce those problems. For release SCM 5.0 this will exist in parallel to the current 6.40 GUI.

Question 15: Key figures in Planning book

"I have created a Planning book with all custom key figures.

I want certain key figures to be input/output and others as output only (so that they are grayed out in the book). When I went into design view of the Planning book (from the planning book) and right clicked on the selected key figure and made it as output only I was surprised to see that all the other key figures also were grayed out (in the sense, the input output key figures that really needs to be made as input key figure was also grayed out). I checked and there is no grouping. Is there any grouping at Planning Book level for key figures?"

A. This sounds like you have issues with your GUI version. You should have the latest SAPGUI patches and SCM Add-on patches. This will solve the problem. (For a detailed explanation please refer to the previous question 14 - Planning book problems)

Question 16: Periodic date Function in Macro

"In my date view I got weekly buckets. I am working on a macro, wherein I need to know the week's placement in a month. The week is either the first of week of the month or the second week of the month. I saw the function which can give me the week's position in a year. However, it does not show the week's position in a month. I tried using both MONTH and WEEK function but did not yield the needed results. How can I derive the requirement of either first or second week of the month?"

A. There is no direct function to calculate this. You might be able to use the macro functions WEEK(),MONTH(),BUCKET_BDATE() and ACT_COLUMN to create a macro that give you the result you need.

Try the sting WEEK {BUCKET_BDATE (ACT_COLUMN)} for the week period requirement. Use a similar formula to place the week within the monthly period requirement. Afterwards, use EVAL to get the desired results from the above two functions.

Question 17: Demand Planning

"We are doing implementation for Demand planning (Version 3.0A).The requirement is, they have seven (7) states for which they want to do forecasting, promotion planning, life cycle planning, etc. for each individual state based on the history data of each one. After which they want to add up the final forecast of all the states and use it for R/3. (There is no connection between R/3 and APO).

The question is, is it feasible to define seven (7) info cubes to have history data for each state and seven (7) Planning books (one for each state) to take the forecast run separately and then add up all these states' final forecast to arrive at a national level forecast? After this, the promotions will be added again at the national level to arrive for a final forecast. This will be downloaded and will be sent to R/3.

Is there a way to make it more feasible or easier to configure rather than doing the run around?"

A. No, you don't need so many InfoCubes. To simplify things and still meet your requirements, instead of having 7 separate InfoCubes for each state, you can have the same results by having a single cube fed from 7 different info sources (if required). You should be able to use one and the same key figure for your 7 histories.

You can then have 7 planning books to control access for each state and as long as you have 'State' as a characteristic. Depending on your design you might actually be able to use the same Planning Book for all 7 states and use the characteristic "State" to control your selections.
Using "State" as a characteristic you also should be able to run only one forecast run or to create exclusive selections for parallel processing.

Finally, you can create one global Planning Book to allow a higher or aggregated view of the combined forecast.

Question 18: Currency Conversion in APO DP

"I want to convert the volume level data into 'Value' by converting the volume into a corresponding value. One way of doing this is by maintaining the conversion factor in the product master and setting the unit of measure in the planning book. But the problem is I want to show value in only one key figure and the rest will all be key figures that should show the volume data only. I also want to show the Key Figure in currency terms by setting the Info object Unit as currency. However, it doesn't display the same way in the planning book and shows the Planning Area UoM as the Key Figure. How can I resolve this?

A corollary question is the standard SAP demo shows value and volume information in the same planning book but I am not able to decipher how they manage to do it. How can I find a way to decipher this function?"

A. Try the following measures:

1) Define the key figure, in which you want to enter values, as a number and not as a quantity UOM for the Info object.
2) While creating the Planning area, in the key figure tab, click details and remove the flag from UOM check box. Next to this will be another column named "Unit of Measure" where you define now the value UOM, e.g. $.
3.) Now write a macro to derive the conversion value .Try to use the macro functions DISPLAY_CONV_FACTOR or UNIT_CONV_FAC, they might pull the conversion factors from the product master into your macro.

You also could try to extract the conversion factor into BW and then load it from there into APO into a key figure. You could then develop a macro that would do the conversion as you need it. Just keep in mind that if you use a price per unit to convert a volume into a value, this price is only valid on a certain level.

If the data 'quantity' is uploaded from a flat file to cube and then to PA, then you can write a small ABAP in the transfer rules to derive the value in another KF and then upload the same to PA.

Question 19: Changing values in a Key figure

"I have a requirement from a user wherein he wants to change the values for the key figure based on a set of drill downs (plant, material and channel). The same key figure is computed by a macro. This is a default macro. Is there a way or a Macro to achieve this? If so, how is the process done?"

A. There are several possibilities how you can combine a drill down function with this default macro so the user would be at the drilldown level where he or she would like to be.

All this will not solve the core of your problem which is the fact that a user wants to enter manually a change to a key figure which is the result of a default macro calculation. This means, as soon as the user confirms the manual input with either "Enter" or "Save" the system will automatically execute the default macro and overwrite the manual input with the macro result.

The only way to solve this dilemma is by using at least 1 additional key figure for the planner to apply his/her changes or inputs. You also would have to modify the default macro to check if there is a value in the manual input key figure. If there is then the default macro has to take the manual value over the calculated one.

Question 20: Year Dependant Fiscal Year Variant in APO DP

"Our client wishes to do demand planning based on a production month calendar. The calendar is based on 12 periods per year with some periods containing 4 weeks while others contain 5 weeks. The start date and end of each period is not the same year to year. For example the "December" production month for 2005 runs from 27 Nov - 31 Dec, whereas the "December" production month for 2006 runs from 3 Dec - 30 Dec. I have created Fiscal year variants for these because the periods are not consistent year to year. I did this through the creation of a year-dependent fiscal year.

So I have managed to create the fiscal year without a problem. However, when I attempt to assign the fiscal year to the Planning Buckets profile, I get the following error:

'Input error 8 in row 1: See long text
Message no. /SAPAPO/MA 840'

Further, I managed to create the Storage buckets profile without a hitch but when I try and create time series objects for the planning area, I get this error:

'Period 2006006 is invalid for periodicity P P1
Message no. /SAPAPO/PRP104'

Diagnosis indicated that the period 2006 is not consistent with periodicity P that was entered in the storage buckets profile for the planning area. What could possibly be done to correct these errors?"

A. These difficulties regarding a fiscal year variant are quiet specific but you definitely can check a couple of things. First you have to make sure that you de-initialized and re-initialized the Planning Area after the Fiscal Year Variant was changed.

Also keep in mind that the Fiscal Year Varian has to be defined one more year on either ends of your initialized horizon of the Planning Area, which means one additional year in the future and one in the past.

This should resolve the problems.

In general, however, I would recommend using the same as Fiscal Year Variant in R/3, if one is part of your system landscape. The Fiscal Year Variant should be maintained in R/3 and then transferred over into APO.

In case you use SNP as well, the use of the Fiscal Year Variant should be synchronized with the SNP team as well.

Question 21: Interactive Demand Planning

"Is it possible to disable the selection window in Interactive Demand Planning? I want the user to work directly with the data selection already created. Bottom line – I don't want the user to load data of his/her choice."

A. Yes, this can be managed with authorizations. Have a look at note 400434 - Authorizations in APO demand planning. I think the object you are looking for is APO_SELID.

Question 22: Data load into APO-DP planning book from Excel

"Is it possible to load data from an Excel file into planning book in version 3.0A? I know this facility was provided in APO 4.0 onwards (readings from sap.com)."

A. The "upload-from-Excel" functionality in APO version 3.0A is really not that great. As far as I know, there is not really a way to load it straight into a Planning Book – unless you want to use a BAPI. I believe the BAPI "PlanningBookAPS" using the methods "GetDetail" and "ChangeKeyfigureValue" might work. This might require, however, a good amount of development work.

There is, however, an 'easy' way to load data into APO using the regular W tools:

1. Create a Data Target with all needed characteristics and key figures.
2. Create a Source System for a PC Flat File.
3. Create a Info source and a Info package.

Now load the Data from the CSV file into the Data Target and use transaction TSCUBE to upload the data from the Data Target into the planning area (DP).

I also would recommend that you evaluate if an upgrade to the latest SCM version is feasible. For example the offline planning functionality in Excel was again dramatically enhanced for SCM 5.0 compared to the SCM 4.x versions.

Question 23: Undoing a liveCache initialization

"Do you know how can I recover the liveCache data after an initialization has been done? Is there any other option besides restoring it from the backup?"

A. In general, you should be very careful when you perform an initialization exactly because of the fact that you will loose all your liveCache data. On the other side, we typically use 2 main ways to ensure the safety of our data: a back-up InfoCube as well as APO system recovery check-points and system back-ups. The settings for the APO system recovery are done by your basis or system administration team. Check with them if you need to have data restored. The downside is that this will restore the data for the whole system, for all users.

It also depends on what was lost. If you lost order data (SNP) and you have a connection to R/3 you can rebuild almost all the results using the CIF and your R/3 connected client.

If it is Demand Planning data that is only in your DP planning area, I hope you have a back up info cube of your planning area. It is because from there, you can reload everything that was lost. If you have not yet made a back-up info cube of your planning area, then I think your best option is a system restore to a back-up.

Question 24: Saving Data in Planning Book SAP APO DP

"Why is the data not saved in the key figure when the disaggregation type is set to "N" (No disaggregation) in the planning area? Each time the 'save' button is clicked in the planning book, the data is lost."

A. By choosing "N" – no disaggregation for a key figure, you basically have turned off the disaggregation. In this case, the only level where you can save data would be at the lowest level. Figure out where your lowest level is and try to save your data there – then it shouldn't be lost anymore.

You can define aggregates on higher levels and try to save data at the level where your aggregate was defined. But watch out, consider the pros and cons of aggregates prior to build them into your system design. OSS note "503363 - Use & management of fixed aggregates in Demand Planning" has some helpful information that you should review.

Question 25: One or more planning areas/book in DP

"I have 10 different countries set up in my system. Each of them has their own demand planners. I have set up a planning area and a planning book for one of them and my idea is to set up identical planning books and areas for the rest. The result will then to produce 10 different planning areas with the same exact structure.

I want to know if that is the best practice (or option), or shall I try to set up just one planning area for all of them? If so, are the users going to be blocked when they start working?"

A. I am sorry but I would not consider your approach as a best practice. I would recommend one planning area/book. You can control who accesses data via the selection profiles. As long as the selection profiles don't overlap, the users will not be able to lock each other out. Another option would be to choosing the characteristic "County" and defining your authorizations based on this characteristic. This involves some minor development but shouldn't be a big deal.

There are some things that you have to look out for though:

1) If there is any change in process requested by a single country it would become difficult to manage considering the fact that all other countries also share the same configuration.
2) Using a single planning area and POS will also increase the CVC's handled and can cause a lag in performance. So make sure you do a proper sizing.
3) The data management will be a bit tricky and functions like realignment (if required) should be handled carefully.
4) Impact of mismanagement (scheduling a wrong background job for instance) would me on higher side with such set of configuration.

Given the above, you can evaluate the pros and cons of both approaches and go from there.

Question 26: APO -DP Inability to track quantity changes in forecasts

"Does anyone know if there is a method to track quantity changes in forecasts? When a person changes an entry in a planning book, the system does not automatically create a historical record of the change. Does anyone know if there is a way to handle the changes?"

A. Indeed, the system does not track changes in Interactive Demand Planning and developing this required function is not necessarily an easy task. I can think right now of two out of many possible solutions, depending on your exact requirement.

If you need to capture the how, what, and when of a forecast change, you'll need audit trail functionality. Although no such functionality exists out of the box, it can be developed using macros. You can create a default macro that validates whether a key figure value has changed. If it does change, you can create an entry in a z-table that records the original value, the new value, the user, and the date (or any other data you might need). Then create a BW report that reports this data.

If you just need to capture the values of all key figures at a periodic interval, extract the planning area contents to an Info Cube. By using a timestamp for the extraction period, you can run reports that compare the values of key figures during points in time. This is normally called a waterfall report.

Question 27: /SAPAPO/TSM 219: Invalid Data Status

"When I try to load a particular product group in the planning book, I am getting the following Error Message. This happens only for 3 product groups but it works fine for the rest of the other product groups:

'/SAPAPO/TSM 219: Invalid Data Status.'

This Error should not occur during normal processing. If it does occur, contact the System Administration or call the SAP Hotline Number.

Application Area: /SAPAPO/TSM
Message No: 219

Is this a functional/configuration/master data problem or does it has something to do with System Administration or support packs?"

A. There are numerous reasons why this can occur. Data inconsistencies in the system are usually the main culprit. The solution will depend on the exact functionality that is causing the message and also your APO release/service pack level.

Usually the consistency check program repairs the LC errors with invalid data status. Run the program /SAPAPO/TS_LCM_CONS_CHECK with the 'Repair' option. Maybe this already will fix your problem.

The best bet for you is to go onto SAP service place and do a notes search on that error message number and then apply the notes that are relevant for your release/patch level. You also might contact your basis team or system administrator for further support.

Question 28: Negative values required for forecasting

"I am using APO to forecast negative values, but I don't see any option in my forecast profiles to allow for negative values. There also seems to be a system setting that automatically changes negative values to zero, which leads me to believe that I can turn it off as well. How do I enable my forecast profiles to allow negative value settings?"

A. To make this clear right from beginning to answer this question, there is no such thing as negative forecasts in APO, simply because is wouldn't be logical to forecast a sales of "-6" products.

The only way a negative forecast could be interpreted would be in customer returns, which in some areas is very important for the business. Even in this case, however, there is no setting you can use in APO to achieve a negative forecast but there are a couple of possible workaround's:

1. You can forecast the customer returns in a separate, positive key figure and then subtract it by using a macro. The downside of this work around is a higher forecast error.
2. If you are working with APO 4.0, you can produce negative values in forecasting MLR using logarithms but your analysis will have to show if you can achieve the desired results.
3. Simply add a great number, e.g. 100,000, to your history to ensure all values are positive prior to forecasting and subtract the same number after. This should then produce a negative forecast which you can read as "customer returns".

Question 29: Forecast in weeks and months

"My time bucket profile is 12 months of which the first three months are in weeks and the rest are indicated in months. The last week of the current month is common between current month and next month.

For example:
> Technically the last day of week 4 of August 2005 is September 2005. How can we make the system consider Aug 31st as the last day of week 4 and Sept 1st as the beginning of the new week?"

A. The solution is quiet simple: You can define a Fiscal Year Variant according to your requirement and associate them it your storage bucket profile. This will produce the results you are looking for.

Question 30: Forecasting profile

"We are now in the process of testing various history data models to see what forecast APO will give us. So far we were not impressed with the auto models. Most of the time, they are just giving us constant models. Meanwhile, the history data clearly shows a trend and/or seasonality.

How we can make the forecast more accurate and reflective of relevant trends to enable the auto models to show it?"

A. Forecast models in APO are just the Statistical tools to help you arrive at a forecast. You basically have to keep playing with the forecast parameters until you achieve the desired forecast accuracy.

In case of Auto Model 2, try the following:
- Use an appropriate forecast horizon (> 2 years) if you are having a 1 year seasonal cycle;
-Clean the data to get rid of the known values of overselling or underselling (Promotions/Stock outs);
-Use APO outlier correction and sigma value of 1.25;

If your data analysis clearly shows that some product groups show a season, trend or trend-seasonal behavior you also should try to group them and create different forecast profiles to accommodate them.

In case if you are not satisfied with the APO forecast values you can also use some external forecast models and bring the data back to APO using the User exits.

Question 31: Tracking of ALERTS

"We have a requirement to see and keep track which Alerts a user has worked on.

For Example: we have 19 alerts and want to see on which alerts (the number of alerts) the user worked on and how many more remaining alerts he/she needs to conclude the work.

How do I track, monitor and identify these alerts?"

A. The alerts have a status which tells you whether they have been processed or not. If you look at the alert monitor screen you will find that there is a prompt whether to accept the alerts or undo it. Therefore, your option is on 'alert' monitor screen. Meanwhile, 'alert' status is stored in a structure. You can easily do a little research and put these all together to fulfill your requirement.

This is the only way how the system will support your efforts to keep track of how many alerts the user has worked through. On the other side is is important to understand that it is also Business Process and Change Management related since the user need to maintain the status field in the Alert Monitor as she/he works through his list of alerts.

Question 32: Parameter conversion error

"How can I resolve the parameter conversion error when running alerts?"

A. I have seen this problem a couple of times but I am afraid to say that solving it was never that easy.
For starters, you can run a consistency check on the alert and then re-activate it. Also review all your alert monitor settings to ensure they are correct. In some cases it might that easy and you are fine.

If this doesn't work, however, you should research the OSS database if this problem can be fixed by applying a note. In case all this doesn't solve your problem you probably have no other choice than opening a OSS message to SAP to have a look at it.

Question 33: Collaborative Demand Planning

"I am working on a Collaborative Demand Planning scenario in APO and need some clarification on the integration process between APO and ITS.

1. We have configured Demand Planning in APO and ITS has been integrated with APO system.

2. We are planning to give the access to external major customers to input and share the data.

How can this be achieved? What are the steps to be followed to achieve this??

A. This simple question will require a lengthy answer, and most of it will probably be done by your basis team.

First you have to complete the following 3 requirements:
1. Maintain the partner settings.
2. Convert the normal DP planning book into a HTML based workbook, including the alerts.
3. Create a collaborative planning workflow.

The second phase of the task is to do a whole of setting changes:

1. Install the Internet Transaction Server (ITS)
Before you begin with the installation, see the ITS documentation provided on the Server Components CD which is delivered together with the software.

In order to display the texts on the initial LOGON screen in the desired language, you must first set the default language in the global ITS data service using ITS parameter ~ language and the language abbreviation of the SAP system.

File Name: global.srvc
Example: ~language EN (for English text display)
Requirement: ITS version 4.6D

2. Publish the Collaborative Planning HTML templates on the ITS server.

Follow the standard procedure for publishing HTML templates together with Internet Application Components (IACs) / Easy Web Transactions (EWT). See the relevant documentation for ITS and SAP@web-studio or ABAP workbench.

The following HTML service templates are required: CLPAMON, CLPBID, CLPGLOBAL, CLPSDP, CLPPROMCAL
The templates can be obtained in the following ways: CAR files /File Name: 30a_apo on SAPSERV3
See OSS Note 327567 (2000)
Check out templates from APO 3.0 system using SAP@web-studio or ABAP workbench (transaction SE80).
See documentation for ITS and SAP@web-studio or ABAP workbench.
You must also install the WEBGUI and MINIALV service templates that come with the ITS installation package.

General settings for Interactive Supply & Demand Planning (for ALL types of data exchange):

Assign a planning book to the user (Demand Planning → Environment → Current Settings → Assign User to Planning Book)

Assign selection profiles to the user (Demand Planning → Environment → Selection Organization → Maintain Selection Assignments)

Settings for drill down in the Internet planning books Maintain the header information of the planning view (Demand Planning → Planning → Interactive Demand Planning → Settings → Header Information).

Choose the characteristics for which you wish to enable drill down and select the Changeable indicator. This setting must be made by the user. Otherwise the settings have no effect.

To display graphic in Internet planning books, you have to maintain the following data under System → User Defaults → Own Data, on the Parameters tab page → Parameter /sapapo/clp_webgraph, value X. In the Internet planning book, you can then show or hide a graphical representation of your data by clicking.

To maintain the settings for notes in Internet planning books, go to System → User Defaults → Own Data on the Parameters tab page: Parameter /sapapo/clp_webnote, value X. In the Internet planning book, you can then click to switch to note mode in order to enter notes on your data. To be able to enter notes, you must use a unique selection (i.e. you must uniquely identify all characteristics).

For the export of data maintain the following data under System → User Defaults → Own Data on the Parameters tab page: Parameter /sapapo/clp_webdown, value:
> XLS (if you want to process the data in Microsoft Excel)
> CSV (if you want to process the data using other software)

Maintain the settings for sorting the data in the case of drill down under System → User Defaults → Own Data on the Parameters tab page: parameter /sapapo/clp_pivot, value X. When you have chosen drill down for a characteristic, you can then switch between the following two displays in the Internet planning book with:
> Sorting of data by key figures

Sorting of data by the drill-down characteristic (e.g. product)

To maintain the settings for header lines in drill down, go to System → User Defaults → Own Data on the Parameters tab page: Parameter /sapapo/clp_rephead, value X. The header line is then shown in the Internet planning book between the objects for which you have chosen drill down.

Choose a drill down by products and maintained the value x for the parameter /sapapo/clp_rephead. The data on the products is then separated by the header line.

For header lines, maintain the following settings under → System → User Defaults → Own Data on the Parameters tab page: Parameter /sapapo/clp_webbhead, value X. The header line is then repeated as a footer line in the Internet planning book.

To maintain the settings for the column width, go to System → User Defaults → Own Data on the Parameters tab page: Parameter /sapapo/clp_row_wi, values S, M, L, XL and ' ' (default). This user parameter enables you to adjust the width of the fixed columns (key figure and characteristic descriptions) in the event of display problems in an Internet planning book.

Do S and M, if you want to display more columns. This may result in the descriptions of the key figures and characteristics being incompletely displayed. Do L and XL, if you need wider columns for more text.

Maintain APO settings for data exchange between planning books. Then, define the time series data exchange.

While APO Customizing for workflow, maintain the following Customizing settings:

→ Create users for external partners
→ Assign user names to the collaboration partners

→ Create a Collaborative Planning Workflow.

→ Supply and Demand Planning via Web access
→ Install the CLP Internet component.

Question 34: APO Reporting

"Does anyone know if there is a way to get at the APO or Live cache database via some sort of reporting tool without having to use BW?

I understand that the mySAP suite of products was designed to have all of the analytics come from BW."

A. If you do not want to use BW at all then there are not too many choices. One way to look at the APO data is to extract it into an InfoCube and read it using list cube. In the bottom line, however, this is still using some BW functionality.

Another way to look at the data would be to use Business Explorer (BeX) which loads on MS Excel - needs to be setup. To avoid the main corporate BW you could use the BeX functionality within APO but again, this is still using BW functionality.

The only way to really not use any other tool would be to extract the data via a BAPI into MS Excel or MS Access. I believe you can use the BAPI "PlanningBookAPS". Once your data is in those external tools, you can use their methods to analyze the data

Question 35: Choosing day in period for LC order in the DP to SNP order

"We have a monthly bucket in DP and SNP. When forecast is transferred from DP to SNP, it is created as one live cache order on the first day of the period covering the month. Is there a way to change the transfer so that the forecast order is on the 3rd or 4th day of the period?

For Example:

>DP 01/2006 forecast 100;
>Transfer to SNP;
>Forecast order created for 01/01/2006;

Instead, we would like it to be created for 01/04/2006."

A. Your observation is correct. If nothing else was done in the system then the released forecast from DP will be created as one liveCache order on the first day of the period in SNP.

As of SCM 5.0 you will have the chance to maintain a distribution function under the current setting of Demand Planning. Here you can define the distribution of your forecast on the days of a month, i.e. in your case that the total forecast will be release to the 3rd day of the period. Next you create a period split profile, where you assign your distribution function.
When you create your release to SNP profile you select your period split profile and the release will take place according to your distribution function.

In previous SCM versions, you can do two things to make the changes:
First option is to check the forecast horizon field in the SNP2 tab of the product master.
The second option is, if you are using CTM and have one forecast a month, change the CTM time stream to weekly and aggregate the forecast to this period via the aggregation tab in CTM. From there, choose the CTM

global configuration setting to middle of the period. CTM will then treat the forecast at the beginning of the month (FI period actually) as if it was on the Wednesday of the first week of the month, instead of Monday.

Question 36: Using Custom KF in Transfer Profiles in DP

"We are using the Custom Key Figure in DP and I am using the same custom characteristic figure in the transfer profile for the transfer of forecast from APO to R/3. It is not getting transferred nor does it throw any error log, and the other settings are fine (Publication types etc).

What I would like to know is if it is possible to use the Custom KF in the transfer profile? Or should we use 9AMATNR only for the transfer of forecast requirements?"

A. To clarify this first, it seems as if terms with different meanings got mixed up in this question. The terms characteristic and key figure are used interchangeable and lead to confusion. I assume, however, that you mean characteristic since he mentions explicit the characteristic 9AMATNR and is getting an error when assigning his own characteristic to the transfer profile.

No, you don't have to use the standard characteristic 9AMATNR for the transfer profile. You can use the custom characteristics to replace product (9AMATNR) and location (9ALOCNO) in APO. However, you have to define those characteristics when you build the MPOS.

You can do this in the Administration of Demand Planning and Supply Network Planning screen (TA: /SAPAPO/MSDP_ADMIN) when configuring the Master Planning Object Structure. On the menu bar, choose EDIT-->Assign Prod/LOC and assign your custom characteristics for product and location. This should resolve your problem.

Supply Network Planning (SNP)

Question 37: Past Due Demands (Backorders) and APO Optimizer

"We just started testing APO Optimizer v4.1 and have the following issue:

'THE OPTIMIZER IS IGNORING PAST DUE DEMANDS'

EXAMPLE: We have a Sales Order with due dates in the past. This shows up in the INITIAL column of the planning table (transaction SNP94). When we run the optimizer, it ignores these Sales Orders (and any other past due demands). This action results in Supply Shortages throughout the entire planning horizon.

Heuristics does consider past due demands. Unfortunately, it does not meet our needs for developing a constrained supply plan.

How can we fix this problem so that the APO optimizer will reflect Past Due Demands (Backorders)?"

A. There are some settings in the optimizer profile that are used when building the model to send to the optimizer. If the demands are not met when sending the optimizer model, a value needs to be passed so that the system can recognize that it is possible to build a pegging link, which can then be analyzed and incorporate a 'waiting' program for possible backorder delays.

But don't confuse these settings with the standard backwards pegging settings in the product master.

Question 38: SNP without DP or PP/DS

"If not using DP and PP/DS, how does SNP Work? I understand that the Demand Plan has to be fed to SNP in order for SNP to do short to mid term planning. I also assume that PPM's came thru PPDS and if not using PPDS, we can use PPMs as APO Master data. If my knowledge of R/3 is accurate, then I further assume that we can transfer the demand plan from R/3 to APO and then execute SNP. However, I am not sure if these assumptions are accurate. Am I on the right track? If not, can I have some inputs so I may adjust accordingly?"

A. In general, APO can be implemented stand alone. If you decided to do so you will have to deal with quiet a bit of interfaces. If you look at the way how the data "flows" through APO then it starts with generating the demand plan in Demand Planning, releasing it to SNP. In SNP you would simulate tactical planning and sourcing decisions before releasing it to PP/DS. You use PP/DS to create procurement proposals to cover the production requirements and to optimize and plan the resource schedule and the order dates/times in detail.

So if you don't plan to use Demand Planning you just have to make sure that you receive your demand plan from an external system. This could be from R/3 or any other tool.
On the other side, if you don't plan to use PP/DS you don't have to either. You can just release your purchase requisitions right back into R/3.

If you have R/3 in place you will transfer the PPM's via the Core InterFace (CIF) into APO. Yes, SNP is using them as well as PP/DS but as I just said, it doesn't mean you have to use both. In case there is no R/3 you always can create your PPM's manually, of course.

Question 39: APO SNP – CTM run produces no result

"My CTM run produces no result. I have created PPM's and assigned them to a model.

I am using standard planning book 9ASNP94. I am able to see my resources having capacity of 8 hours a day and also initial demand with stock on hand for my products.

I didn't make many changes to the CTM engine (all I mentioned is VERSION) and selected all master data. The log does not show any errors.

What could be the problem?"

A. The main part about any of the three solvers that SNP has to offer (Heuristics, CTM and Optimizer) is that they are very master data intensive – and that this master data need to be set up correct.

My experience has shown that if a CTM run doesn't produce a result in many cases there is at least setting not complete or incorrect maintained. You should review your settings as well as checking your master data selection. Keep in mind that a incorrect master data selection reflects no errors in evaluation and yet does not produce any planning results of a CTM run either.

Question 40: Complex Setup time calculation

"We are trying to figure out how to handle a complex calculation of setup times. We are working in a metal mill industry and setup times depend on dimensions. This means that setup is a very big factor for increasing width, but zero for decreasing width. As far as I know it is not possible to model something like that using setup groups and setup keys because this could lead to an infinite number of combinations. If you also consider thickness or other characteristics like color and even process characteristics like temperature, then the whole thing gets too complicated to handle via setup keys. How can I find a simpler method to approach this and fulfill the requirement of setting up a program that will automatically set up complex time calculations?"

A. You might be interested in some SCM 5.0 developments where the system can generate its own composite matrices based on matrices that you enter for swaps between individual characteristic evaluations. And I don't mean setup groups, I do mean characteristic evaluations. In this development, you can maintain a setup matrix for setup swaps between thickness characteristics, and another for length.

The system can then generate a composite matrix that will have many more entries (but it saves you from doing it), and it's possible to specify that the composite swap should either be the max, sum or Badi dependent value with regard to the individuals.

The system also generates its own 'setup group' which it applies to the order that can then be used to build the swap time for the order in planning.

There are some restrictions, and you'll need to contact SAP to get some consulting if you are interested in taking it further.

Question 41: Product Interchange

"We have activated product interchangeability function. We want to have a range of substitution (one to many or vice versa). For example: A -> B, C ->B with different validity from date. Currently, system is not permitted when we create substitution C->B. It states: 'Error occurred: Interchangeability not continuous'.
What does this mean?"

A. It almost sounds as if you encountered this error because the assumptions you made are not supported by the system design. As a matter of fact, PP/DS only supports linear super session chains. In a linear super session chain, each product in the super session chain can have only one predecessor and one successor. The products in a super session chain are therefore linked by 1:1 relationships. Supersession chains in which a product has several successor products (1:N), or several products have one successor product (N:1) are not permitted.

Question 42: Creating PPMs in APO

"I am trying to create PPM's in APO but then I am not able to understand as to how to satisfy this requirement. Is there a way to create PPM's manually in APO without getting anything transferred from R/3?"

A. Yes, of course there is a way to create PPM's in APO manually. You do have to make sure, however, that you have the products, the locations, and the resources created first in APO before you can create a plan (PPM). It is the prerequisite for a PPM that the master data exists.

If you keep this in mind, you should be able to create a PPM without any big problems. Just be sure you really meant to create a PPM and not a PDS (Production Data Structure). PDS' can only be generated by CIF and not be modified or changed in APO. In APO you only can delete them.

Question 43: Stock in transit

"How to reflect the values in "In Transit" key figure of planning book for SNP (std). I have two locations - one is shipping location A and the other one is receiving location B.

I have created an STO IN TLB from A location and created GI. Delivery from location A STO disappeared from the location A. But I am not seeing any values in key figure in transit at location A OR B. I have an integration model for stock in transit active. How do I fix this?"

A. You must create an inbound delivery at the receiving location (B) for the stock to show up being in transit. The inbound delivery is SAP's standard way of showing it in transit.

Question 44: Loading Purchase info into liveCache

"I have been asked to load SNP data (purchase orders) into APO 3.10 from a flat file so that the client can view it in the Planning Book [Live] SNP interactive planning/SNO plan TCODE - /SAPAPO/SDP94.

Is this possible? If so, how could is this accomplished?"

A. Yes, this is can be accomplished and you have the choice between the following two options:
My first choice option would be to load them into the planning area as time series key figures and proceed from there. This is probably the most cost effective way.
The second method requires quiet a bit more effort. You can upload the information using a BAPI - BAPI_POSRVAPS_SAVEMULTI2. This can be used for the purpose but you would need the help of an ABAPer to do the task.

Question 45: Conversion of PP/DS PPM to SNP PPM

"I am encountering complications when converting a PP/DS PPM to an SNP PPM – that is, the primary resource is not getting carried over. When I look at the SNP mode, there is duration but the Primary Resource field is blank.

The resource in question is Multimixed, and the "Not SNP Relevant" flag is not checked.

After further investigation, I called up the PP/D PPM and did a "check plan" - which gave me several errors...namely "no bucket consumption maintained for resource"....or something to that effect.

What could be causing these errors? How can these be corrected?"

A. When the PP/DS PPM converts to a SNP PPM, it is the bucket consumption that it uses not the variable consumption that shows. You will need to add this in your PP/DS PPM.

Question 46: Changing PPM's thru BAPI_PPMSRVAPS_SAVEMULTI_30A

"I want to change existing PPM's by using BAPI_PPMSRVAPS_SAVEMULTI_30A. After setting up the itabs and calling the BAPI and the necessary COMMIT WORK everything looks fine (return - table is empty). However, the values to be changed stay unmodified (checked through /SAPAPO/SCC03-transaction). With the debugger, I could find out a place in the source code where a flag is queried whether COMMIT WORK should be done inside the BAPI - after switching it on (= COMMIT WORK inside the BAPI) the new value was set and showed up in SCC03! Is there any way to turn this flag on programmatically?"

A. You might want to try these two options. First, if you wanted to change a field the capacity requirements structure should indicate:
> *" CAPACITY_REQ STRUCTURE BAPI10003REQCAP OPTIONAL

You would also need to set an X in the corresponding entry of the additional structure (below):
> *" CAPACITY_REQ_X STRUCTURE BAPI10003REQCAPX OPTIONAL

Second, even though the German documentation of parameter PPM reads as if for every entry in PPM a corresponding entry in capacity_req is needed, independent of whether the capacity_req shall be changed or not, you should ignore this for your purpose. Try to leave out the capacity_req and capacity_req_x – tables and the changes to the PPMs should be accepted by the BAPI and written to the database.

Question 47: SNP Optimizer take a lot of time running

"I'm running the SNP optimizer and the solution is ok at the end, but it takes a long time in order to get the solution (around 6 hours).

We are running the optimizer for some like 4,000 SNP orders with 2 level components.

Besides to check only the required parameters in the Optimizer, what else can I do in order to shorten the planning run time?"

A. The running time depends on the optimization technique you are using. Linear is usually quicker than discretization. If you are using discretization, then the more discrete functions you use, the longer it will take. I recommend no more than 2.

Also, and this is something you can always try with all your background processing jobs, you should see if you can apply parallel processing for the background Optimizer run. This usually reduces the total run time a lot and gives results much faster.

Question 48: SNP standard planning areas issues

"I encountered some issues while doing SNP standard planning areas:

1) The default UOM assigned to 9ASNP02 is PC, we don't use that unit of measure. What is the best option to go about it? I need to create a new planning area of 9ASNP02.

2) When we initialize 9ASNP02 it doesn't ask for a date from and to, like it does for 9ASNP01. Is this normal?

3) Initialization of 9ASNP01 takes a long time while 9ASNP02 is done in a few minutes. Why so?"

A. The responses are numbered accordingly:

1.) Yes. Create a copy of the 9ASNP02 planning area and change the default UoM.

2.) Yes, this is normal since the planning area 9ASNP02 is an order based planning area and therefore doesn't require a time series like 9ASNP01.

3.) This is related to the generation of time series (see response to number 2).

Question 49: Dynamic pegging

"How do we change the dynamic pegging relationship interactively?
My problem is I have stocks dynamically pegged to say sales order no 1.
Later on I have a sales order no. 2 which is to be confirmed and delivered before sales order no 1. The system doesn't confirm any quantities due to the fact that the quantities are dynamically pegged to sales order no1.

How can I change the dynamic pegging relation?"

A. Maybe the change from dynamic to fixed pegging would solve your problems. You can do it from the product view. Double click on element to go to details. Over there you can see the details of pegging relationship, and you can also see alternatives for pegging, which you can fix.

If that doesn't solve your problem it might be that this is not a pegging issue, but an ATP issue. If the above does not work for you, try using Tcode /SAPAPO/BOPI to switch confirmation from one order to another (If you are using Global-ATP, otherwise you should use CO06 in R/3).

Question 50: Stock in transit Upload

"Can anyone tell me what BAPI or RFC can be used to upload Stock in transit data from the External source?"

A. Take BAPI_GOODSMVT_CREATE plus an integration model.

Stock would be entered into the R/3 system via a goods movement created by the above BAPI and an integration model would transfer the stock information to APO.

Question 51: Changing a resource in a Heuristic

"I am using a Customer Heuristics in which I change the resource for a specific order operation before the Function "/SAPAPO/EFPL_ONLINE_SCHEDULER" is called.

When I debug the Function I noticed it calls another Function "/SAPAPO/OM_ACT_SCHEDULE". This function in turn connects to Live Cache & calls the stored procedure "SAPAPO_PT_ACT_SCHEDULE2" with the changed resource data. However, it schedules the order operation with the wrong resource.

I assume that the stored procedure uses the resource data found in Live Cache and not the data passed to it by the last Function.

How do I solve this problem?

My first guess is to change the order prior to calling the "/SAPAPO/EFPL_ONLINE_SCHEDULER" Function.

What function do I use (if at all) to change the order?"

A. This is a hard to answer question since it is a custom Heuristics and without knowing all the changes to the coding this is a question for either the developer who developed the code originally or for an ABAPer to debug the code and see what is going on.

Master Data

Question 52: APO DP planning book upload type

"I have to upload data in the DP planning book from a legacy system. The different options available regarding the update type from this field are as follows:

OW1 - Overwrite Completely, First Period distribution
OW2 - Overwrite Completely, Consistent distribution
PW1 - First: Overwrite partially Period Distribution
PW2 - Overwrite partially: Consistent Distribution
DL1 - Delta Update: First Period Distribution
DL2 - Delta Update: Consistent Distribution

My question is where can I find the PUPDATE field in APO to specify the nature of update type for the DP planning book?"

A. A possible approach for a possible solution that jumps into my mind would be the following:
First change the template:
/SAPAPO/TS_PSTRU_SAMPLE_MD_GEN in order to load with zeros. Secondly, us the flag [X] Ignore zero values, and last update the values in table RSSGTPCLA.

As said above, this is a non-standard solution and I do highly recommend researching this as well as other possible solutions with your team and some developers.

Question 53: Deleting product master from APO

"How can I mass permanent delete product master (not just set the deletion flag) from APO? I have tried to use BDC and done /sapapo/mat1> Mark for deletion but the result comes out to set the deletion flag as supposed to permanent delete when you do it manually. Is there another way to do it?"

A. After setting the deletion flag try the report to delete product master. Try this menu path:

> Master Data → Product Master → "Delete Products" off the Extras tab within the Product Master.

Question 54: Classification view of Product master in APO

"We would like to use the Characteristics in the Classification view of the product master in APO. Normally, when I create a characteristic in R/3 and attach it to a class within the classification view of the Material master, the relevant characteristic will be displayed out - of which I can select a value.

For example:

If my Characteristic is color that I have attached to a class, when this class is called in the Classification view of the Material master, the Characteristic is called in which I can either select RED or YELLOW etc. But in APO, I have done the same thing by creating a Characteristic, attaching it to a Class. However, when I called the Class in Classification view of the product master and clicked the details icon, I see only the Characteristic Name (but not the values) which means that I cannot assign a value to that particular part number (product) in APO.

I am not sure where I went wrong in any step. How do I determine where I went wrong and how can I fix this?

Note that I have tried transferring the Class & Characteristics using CIF - that too didn't work. We are in APO3.1."

A. You need to maintain the Customizing in R/3 and the same in APO since these customizing settings are not CIFed throughout the Integration models.

You need to enter the organizational area at the level of the Class and at the level of individual characteristic identifying it as those that are supposed to go to APO.
In APO, select the table /SAPAPO/MATKEY and choose Organizational Areas. Choose 'new Entries' to create organizational areas. If you have not maintained these settings,

the system will still transfer but you may not be able to display the input.

BASIS

Question 55: No AUTOLOG File

"We have installed SCM 4.1 on windows 64 bits (live cache 7.5).
I noted that there is no AUTOLOG file on operating system.

I have defined AUTOLOG Medium and it is in status AUTOLOG
ON, but there is no file on operating system.

DEVLog is 2GB and LOG_SEGMENT_SIZE is 85333.
I think there is not a lot of activity on this system (it is not yet in
production life).

But why there is no file on operating system?
Must I reduce LOG_SEGMENT_SIZE?
What problem could it generate?
I do a DATA backup one time by day and LOG backup 3 times by
day.
I think when I do a LOG backup (and stop AUTOLOG before and
restart it after), the log is empty? (And data are put in DATA?)
So may be it is normal there is no file in AUTOLOG.

Is it a problem for a restoration of warm backup??

A. At first you should check that the LOG is actually on. You
only will get a log when the LOG is filled or if you force it to write
it in logs. To do so, use the "on" command:
      DBMCLI -d LCA -u control, control -uUTL -c autolog_off
      DBMCLI -d LCA -u control, control -uUTL -c autolog_on

To force the system now to switch the log, try to create a media:
      dbmcli -u control, control medium_put LOGS X:\LOGS
      FILE LOG 0 8 YES

Then start backup on disk and it hopefully solves your problem:
      DBMCLI -d LCA -u control, control -uUTL -c autolog_off

DBMCLI -d LCA -u control, control -uUTL -c
backup_start LOGS
DBMCLI -d LCA -u control, control -uUTL -c autolog_on

Question 56: Stop liveCache versus stopSAP

"My question is regarding the activation of a parameter change in liveCache.

Will stopping (stopSAP ALL) SAP have the same effect as stopping liveCache to activate the parameter change? Or is it entirely different?

Do changes to liveCache parameters require stop&start of the liveCache only? Can it possibly be activated even after a stopSAP?"

A. If you restart just the liveCache, then that is all you do - restart the Live cache.

If you do a 'stopSAP ALL' then it depends:
>As of SCM 4.0, then everything is stopped, including liveCache. However, be careful with earlier SCM/APO versions - only the app server and underlying database (i.e. oracle) is actually stopped – the liveCache is still there.

You should have no reason to restart the whole system just to activate some liveCache parameter changes. Simply use the functionality in LC10. It is also safer than using the DBMGUI (especially with older liveCache / APO versions).

Question 57: Live Cache to APO tables

"I need to know if there is a function modules/BADI that reads the data from Live cache to APO tables.

For Example:
How does the SA line derive from the Live cache and stored in transparent table?"

A. This is a question that should be addressed primarily to a developer. Others, like a consultant or a system administrator might just have not the ABAP background and experience that is needed to properly answer the question.
In general, COM routines are called from ABAP function modules to perform actions on any liveCache data, which is stored in the object oriented data areas. For all other (relational) data you should be able to use native SQL calls.

If you want to view the liveCache data you might be able to use transaction SAPAPO/OM16.

Question 58: Connection between liveCache & BW

"We have separate liveCache server, APO server and BW server. The process we follow now is that after running different programs in liveCache for Demand Planning, we load the data to a cube (say cube xyz) in the APO server for back up of the liveCache data. We then load the data from cube xyz from the APO server to a cube in BW server for reporting.

Is there a way to load data directly from the Live cache to BW, without loading the APO server? If yes, what do I need to do in Live cache to set up the connection to BW?

A. If you intend to connect liveCache directly to the BW system instead of saving the planning results into the local APO system first before copying them across to the remote cube, then No, you definitely can't do that!!!

Question 59: Live cache returns error 4016 when executed

"Live cache returns error – '4016 An SQL error occurred' when executed (while /SAPAPO/OM03).

It seems that live cache installation program do not create procedures in MaxDB and are not initialized properly. Is it possible to somehow initialize them manually? How do I create a clear installation procedure?

I am currently using Platform win64, live cache version 7.4..., SCM version 4.1.
Is it easier to install & run it on win32?"

A. The best way to resolve this is to check initialization log and go from there. However, since you have SCM4.1 which is supported only with Live Cache 7.5, you'll have difficulty doing this even if attempted on win32. An upgrade review maybe in order to resolve the issue.

Question 60: SAP SCM Components

"As far as I know SAP SCM has APO, EM and ICH as its components. However, when I checked with on-service.sap.com, it gave this list?

1. Demand and Supply Planning
2. Service Parts planning
3. Procurement
4. Manufacturing
5. Warehousing
6. Order Fulfillment
7. Transportation
8. Analytic
9. Supply Chain Event management
10. Supply Chain collaboration

I can understand that these are the processes in any supply chain. But are these all part of mySAP SCM 4.0?"

A. The SCM portal in SAPNet views the Supply Chain Management as the combination of the SCM components and the R3 Logistics components working together. That is the reason why when you open Procurement you get a link to Materials Management.

APO itself contains the following parts:
    Demand Planning (DP)
    Supply Network Planning (SNP)
    Production Planning/ Detailed Scheduling (PP/DS)
    (TP/VS)
    global Available to Promise (gATP)

As of release SCM 4.0, APO was bundled with ICH (Inventory Collaboration Hub) and EM (Event Management).

The Forecast and Replenishment Engine (F&RE) was added to the SCM suite with release SCM 4.1. Keep in mind that the F&R engine is designed to work with the SAP R/3 Retail solution.

The latest addition will be Spare Parts Planning (SPP) with SCM 5.0.

CoreInterFace (CIF)

Question 61: Change Planned Orders to Production Orders

"I was trying to convert planned orders created in APO to production orders in R/3. I have placed the transfer indicator in the orders and when I execute the transaction for transfer it says transfer has taken place but I still cannot find the orders in R/3. How do I effect the change?"

A. If you have the integration model in place, proceed to check the R/3 inbound and outbound queues for any blocks.

You also have to keep in mind that the R/3 conversion to process orders would have caused a change in the order number so you can't find the same order number in R3.

Question 62: How to CIF the PPM without operations

"We have setup a subcontracting flow. However, I need to plan it in APO. I need to start from a DP forecast, in PPDS to create a subcontracted PR (I have the subcontracted info record in APO) I need a PPM with the BOM. But, I can't CIF the BOM (Production Version) since it doesn't contain an operation. Must a PPM always contain an operation? I don't need that operation in APO, for the simple reason that there are no activities (except for the handling), and the service cost is in the info record. I would like to know what the best way is to go about it.

Should I create a dummy WorkCenter, and some dummy activity, just for the sake of being able to CIF the PPM?"

A. First of all, yes, you do need an operation to be able to CIF it into APO, even if you don't need it there. In that sense also a yes for your second question, you will have to proceed to create a dummy, infinite resource and a master recipe with 1 phase with a fast duration, for example 1,000/hr.

As the PPM is used for the BOM explosion, the details of the task list are irrelevant in APO.

Question 63: Location transfer via CIF

"We have a new plant and we are trying to CIF to APO at CFM2 system. It is showing the error 'Location does not exist for external location number EF00, type 1001, BSG'. How do we correct this error?"

A. Two ideas what you can do. First thing to do is to make sure you assigned the correct logical system (R/3) to a business system group. Secondly, check the Planning version attached to the plant. It should be set to '000'.

Question 64: No vendor "cifed" to APO?

"We have set all configurations for the integration between APO and R/3. We are absolutely sure that there is no issue there. We did now define an Integration Model to "cif" over the vendors into APO.
When we checked in APO, however, the vendor wasn't there even though we received the message that it was transferred successfully. We went and checked the log files on R/3 side as well as in APO but all lights were on green. What went wrong and how can we "cif" our vendors over into APO? "

A. There are basically only 2 answers to this problem. The first thing you should recall is the fact that vendors will have leading "0" (zeros) once they are in APO. This is the same as for customers. So try to find the vendor in the location master in APO and also type in the leading "0". Especially if you don't use the CIF very often this might be a detail you might have not thought of.

If you have verified that all settings are correct and all log files are green and that there is no vendor in APO (even if you type the leading zeros) then there is probably no easy answer and you should probably open a message to SAP. In some cases it also can be that your IT support organization might have resources that are able to resolve the problem.

Question 65: APO relevance

"I am getting one warning message saying that 'work center/resource is not APO relevant while creating integration model'. What does this mean?"

A. During the transmission of the PPM, every operation of routing is checked. If a work center does not have a control key, which shows that it is relevant for both, capacity planning and scheduling, and both formulas are maintained in the work center to calculate capacity demand and scheduling time, the system tells you that it is not relevant for APO.

Question 66: Extending selection conditions for production orders in cfm1

"The selection conditions for production orders do not meet my requirements when the integration model was generated. I am aware that OSS Note 507696 can be used to extend the selection criteria for MARC fields in 'cfm1'. But information regarding this is not readily available in the production order selection. Is there a way to extend the selection criteria for production orders (i.e. with order type AUART)? If utilizing a user exit, which one?"

A. This is a really specific question. For the first question on extending the selection criteria for production orders, I am not aware of such functions to comply with the requirement. For the second query, you can try the user exit CIFORD02 with ZXCIFU07 if they help you achieve your goal but without further information and investigation it is hard to say if they are the right ones. I certainly do suggest that you research the problem thoroughly with a developer.

Question 67: The integration model in cfm1

"I am trying to transfer a plant from R/3 to APO but while doing so, I am getting the error:
'Error when creating address of location -- type Production plant'.

I have checked the address of the plant in R/3 but I didn't find anything wrong with it. What can be the problem and how do I resolve it?"

A. Typically an error message like this can have many different causes and there are several ways to approach this issue. The most common ones that you should check are:

1) Have you copied the same factory calendars you are using in R/3 to APO? If they do not exist in APO it will not create the location.

2) Check the Time Zones. Ensure consistency between R/3 and APO.

3) This is a slight possibility - do you have Geo-coding set? If so, have you given the Plant the correct level to define the Geo-code in APO?

4.) Check up the region code in the location R/3. If there are special characters 'o' with a dot on top, then the plant can not be transferred to APO. There is a BW setting to permit that.

5.) Depending on your IMG setting, it may be that a postcode is a required field in the location master and if not maintained, this might give you the error you get. Type in transaction "spro", go to mySAP SCM IMG → General Settings → Set Country specific check and check if the flag if set or not, Make sure your location master data is maintained accordingly.

Question 68: Transferring data from R/3 to APO

"I was trying to transfer data from R/3 enterprise to APO 4.0. However, even though I have inferred from help.sap.com, I still wasn't able to do this function successfully. How do I transfer data from R/3 to APO?"

A. A generic description of how you transfer data can only be on a high level since there is not much detailed information and requirement details mentioned in your question. In general, perform the following steps:

4. 1. Create integration models for master data and transaction data

2. Activate the integration models and select CFM1.
3. Enter the model name→ select the logical system → select APO application.

Then, select each master data and enter the relevant data for each master data.
4. After creating the model go to CFM2 to activate the model.
5. Enter the model, logical system, and the APO application.
6. Execute the transaction.

After these, you will get the model in that page. You can now select the model and activate it.

Take note that you can create location in APO or you can make one integration model for location by selecting plant in CFM1.

Question 69: CIF - Transferring Sales Orders from R/3 to APO

"I am trying to transfer sales orders from R/3 to APO. I am able to transfer purchase orders, but not sales orders.

Once I activate the Integration Model in R/3, I am not able to see the sales order in R/3 that has to be transferred to APO.

I am looking at the right place in APO for the transferred sales orders (/SAPAPO/RRP3 - Product View). What could be the reason why sales order cannot be viewed?"

A. You need to check some items on this:

2. First you should check whether the integration model is active. This is an easy guess but sometimes it is the easy steps that get forgotten.

1. If #1 didn't solve the problem, you should check your outbound queue in R/3 and inbound queue in APO. You will get more explanation there. May be some master data or UOM may be missing. Check the queue errors first.

Question 70: Assigning characteristic value for PPM's via CIF

"I'm trying to find a way to automatically assign characteristics to the PPM's when CIF occurs. How can this be done?"

A. I am not sure if I got this problem all right but it sounds as if you are talking about the maintenance of the characteristic propagation (CDP) for PPM plans, which is usually only possible interactively. In simple cases where only standard valuations are used in PPM, these can also be enhanced during the initial transfer of PPM plans via user exits on the APO side. This is described in OSS note 495825.

Production Planning – Detailed Scheduling (PP/DS)

Question 71: PPDS quantity alerts

"I found the results of the PPDS quantity alerts to be difficult to interpret in a real time business situation. Is there a way for these alerts for receipts and requirements to be programmed so as to reflect actual shortage and surplus in terms of percentages?"

A. The PPDS alerts are based on the pegging situation of the requirements and receipts. You can change the pegging windows and the alert windows mode on the demand tab/pegging sub tab. This will change the results significantly.

In general, set a broad range on the pegging limits that lets the receipts peg to the requirements. Afterwards, set the alert limits to see if things are late or early. This should take care of your concern.

Question 72: Blocked stock in APO

"We are implementing APO 3.1 with SAP R/3 4.7. Blocked stock is not recognized in APO 3.1 as available stock. I know that it is recognized in 4.x but we can't upgrade to 4.x at present. So, I am looking for some help. How do I resolve the blocked stock in 3.1?"

A. You can use the exit described in note 487166 and 566642 for enhancement of APOCF011. This might help to solve your problem.

Question 73: Product Planning Table set up

"I'm working with APO 3.0. Using transaction /SAPAPO/PPT1 (Product planning table) on screen "Product view: periodic" some PlOrd rows are modifiable (input/output) while some are not (output only). The PPM's are different. PlOrd-s with input possibility connects to different resources than others. I want to modify all PlOrd quantity. What is missing here?"

A. Check the resource operating time assigned to resource. The planed orders connecting to the resource are used as output only in the planning table if no time is assigned.

Question 74: Automatic Production Planning monitoring

"We will be going live with APO PP/DS in a couple of weeks and are now in the middle of automating most of our activities. Is there list of jobs that is elementary to have for PP/DS?"

A. There are certain jobs that must be scheduled on a regular basis to ensure correct and current production planning

Report /SAPAPO/BACKGROUND_SCHEDULING performs the different processing steps necessary for the production planning run.

Report /SAPAPO/SAPRRPLOG_DELETE deletes the PP/DS log, which must be deleted regularly to maintain the high performance of the related transactions.

Depending on your scenario, you might choose to run report /SAPAPO/AMON_MAIL_BROADCAST to send alert monitor mails.

To determine the alerts in the background you must schedule the report /SAPAPO/READ_ALERTS_BATCH as a periodical batch job.

Using the report /SAPAPO/AMON_REORG you can delete alerts in the alert monitor that are older than a specified date. As of SCM Release 4.0, this is also relevant for PP/DS since it is possible to use database alert types as well.

You also should remember to schedule the necessary jobs for the maintenance of the application log. You can delete obsolete application jobs using report SBAL_DELETE. Keep in mind that a log only can be deleted when it has reached its expiry date of if it has the "Deletion before expire" flag set.

On the R/3 side, you can use report RDELBALS to delete obsolete application log search index entries.

Besides those jobs you have to make sure that of course all the general jobs that should run regularly on an APO system are scheduled. Those, however, are not PP/DS specific.

Transport Planning – Vehicle Scheduling (TP/VS)

Question 75: TPVS Inconsistencies and cancellation of jobs

"I have finished my transportation planning and want to publish them so the subsequent process steps can be triggered. When it comes to that point, however, there seems to be an inconsistency or an error in the publishing that caused the cancellation of the batch job.

Can anybody give advice on how to find the problem?"

A. First of all, I am not sure if the cancellation of the job as you describe it is really caused by an inconsistency or by an error. Either way, there are a couple of things you can try.

Use the TP/VS consistency check tool (/SAPAPO/VSCC) to find inconsistencies within the different database tables. With this job you can not only detect publishing related inconsistencies but also other areas, customizing and R/3 settings.

You should then try to publish again and see if the job still cancels. If so then this means there are errors and you should use the transaction /SAPAPO/VS54 for the shipment deletion after you have run /SAPAPO/VSCC.

Question 76: Delivery and Shipment deletion

"We are up and running with TPVS for a while now and the entries for executed deliveries and shipments are filling up our system. What should we do to gain again control over this problem?

A. You need to understand first that deliveries that are on a shipment at goods issue/receipt posting are not deleted. Their quantities are reduced to 0 instead. In order to avoid a liveCache overflow, however, old deliveries with quantities of 0 that are no longer on shipments must be deleted. To do so, you should schedule the transaction 'SAPAPO/VS53 ideally on a daily basis.

On the other side, the shipments that receive status END are posted to an exclusion table and the database entries receive a deletion flag. For deleting the old shipments you should schedule the transaction /SAPAPO/VS54 ideally on a daily basis as well.

These two jobs should help you to control your system.

Question 77: Carrier Selection: Call into R/3 can't be completed

"As an additional scenario for our TPVS we want to use the carrier selection function. We already performed some testing but for some reasons it seems that the call into R/3 to check on the rated can't be completed.

How can we fix this or is there a workaround?

A. Did you already run transaction /SAPAPOVSCC to check on possible inconsistencies between the carrier selection tables in TPVS and the allocations? If you are lucky, you might already find the problem there and if not it is always good to know that the data is consistent.

I almost do expect, however, that the consistency check tool will not find anything. So if the call into R/3 for the check on the rated can't be performed, you should use the internal costs instead.

global Available to Promise (gATP)

Question 78: ATP Horizon

"Any idea where we can define the ATP horizon? For example, the period for which ATP check would be carried out. I believe it must be somewhere while initializing the ATP time series. Where can I find this function and how should we go about it?"

A. The ATP Checking Horizon is defined per product/location combination in the Checking Horizon Field on the product master. Define the horizon here and remember to use an ATP Group that takes the horizon into account.

Question 79: Temporary Quantity Assignments

"During our gATP execution we have observed that some quantities are locked and we are unable to confirm those quantities even though we actually should be able to confirm them.

Can someone advise on how to resolve this situation since this causing some severe situations in our production system."

A. Sometimes in can happen – and in your case it seems like it – that Temporary Quantity Assignments (TQA) still exist in APO even though they are not longer being used. It is recommended to delete these old TQA's periodically because if not done it can cause the problems you have described.

You can use the transaction /SAPAPO/AC06 to monitor and delete the Temporary Quantity Assignments. Another way to deleted them is using the report /SAPAPO/OM_DELTA_REMOVE_OLDER. TQA's that are caused by backorder processing are deleted via /SAPAPO/BOP_DELETE.

Please ensure that only those TQA's are deleted that are caused by processed that are finished.

Question 80: Exact ATP date in APO

"Is it possible in APO to know the exact ATP date on getting an enquiry from a customer for supply of a product, considering the following

1. Available capacity.
2. Production lead time of Finished product (including its sub-assemblies).
3. Availability of components required (If the required components are not available, then system should consider procurement lead time of these components and from the availability date of components, it should calculate the production time of the product)
4. System should also consider the alternative production facilities if available.

If possible, through which components of APO we can achieve it?"

A. You can realize those requirements using the CTP concept in APO. This is basically a combination of gATP and PP/DS.

You should be aware, however, that there are many pitfalls and restrictions in this area. In other words, you will have to be quite creative to make this work since it is not an SAP-out-of-the-box delivered solution for fulfill your needed.

Some of the issues you probably will run into:
> "to the second scheduling" vs. ATP buckets
> CTP planning heuristic vs. planning heuristic used in planning run
> low resource utilization by gaps in scheduling
> getting the integration with R/3 to work

My advice is to carefully review all your needs and see if you have to go this route or if there are other ways to get to your goals.

Event Manager (EM)

Question 81: SCEM Triggers

"What transaction is used to change the configuration of event handlers? How do I set the triggers of the event handlers to be inactive?"

A. This is not to hard. Go to SPRO → Integration with other mySAP.com Components → Event Management Interface → Define Application interface → Define SAP EM interface functions. From there, you can set the triggers of the event handler.

Index

Transactions

Transactions within SAP SCM:

SPRO – IMG Customizing start screen (→ button "SAP Reference IMG)

/SAPAPO/SCC02 - Supply Chain Cockpit
/SAPAPO/AMON1 - Alert Monitor
/SAPAPO/AMON_SETTING - Set Alert Monitor

/SAPAPO/SDP94 – Interactive Demand Planning
/SAPAPO/CLPISDP - Collaborative Demand Planning
/SAPAPO/MP34 – Promotion Planning
/SAPAPO/MP39 – Promotion Reporting
/SAPAPO/MP42 - Promotion Management

/SAPAPO/MC8T - Define Activities for Mass Processing
/SAPAPO/MC8D - Create Demand Planning in the Background
/SAPAPO/MC8G - Schedule Demand Planning in the Background
SM37 – Job Overview of Demand Planning in the Background
SM36 – Schedule Background Job

/SAPAPO/MC90 – Release Demand Planning to Supply Network Planning
/SAPAPO/REL_TO_SNP - Release InfoProvider to Supply Network Planning
/SAPAPO/REL_TO_OLTP - Release InfoProvider to SAP R/3

/SAPAPO/MSDP_ADMIN – Administration of Demand Planning and Supply

Network Planning

/SAPAPO/MC62 – Maintain Characteristic Values

/SAPAPO/TSCOPY – Copy/Version Management

/SAPAPO/TSCUBE – Load Data from InfoCube

RSA1 – BW Administrator Workbench

RSPC - Maintain Process Chains

/SAPAPO/RLGCOPY - Data Realignment - Realignment

/SAPAPO/SDP8B - Define Planning Book

/SAPAPO/ADVM - Macro Workbench

/SAPAPO/TR30 - Maintain Time Buckets Profile for Demand Plng and

Supply Planning

/SAPAPO/TR32 - Periodicities for Planning Area

/SAPAPO/MC7B - Product Split

/SAPAPO/MC7A - Location Split

/SAPAPO/MSDP_SB - Safety Stock Planning

/SAPAPO/SNP94 – Interactive Supply Network Planning

/SAPAPO/SNPFCST – Release SNP-Confirmed Forecast to Demand

Planning

/SAPAPO/SNPSOP - Sales & Operations Planning (SOP)

/SAPAPO/CLPISDP - Collaborative Supply Planning

/SAPAPO/SDP94 – Interactive Supply Network Planning (all Books)

/SAPAPO/SNPTLB - Transport Load Builder (TLB)

/SAPAPO/CTM - Capable-to-Match (CTM)

/SAPAPO/SNPOP - Supply Network Optimization

/SAPAPO/SNP05 - Capacity Leveling

/SAPAPO/SNP01 - Supply Network Planning in the
Background
/SAPAPO/SNP02 – Deployment

/SAPAPO/SNPAPLOG - Application Logs
/SAPAPO/SNPOPLOG - Optimizer Log Data

/SAPAPO/VERMER - Planning Version Merge
/SAPAPO/RLCDEL - Delete Transaction Data
/SAPAPO/LCOUT – Release to Demand
Planning
/SAPAPO/SNPFCST - Release SNP-Confirmed
Forecast to Demand
Planning

/SAPAPO/BOPI - Interactive Backorder Processing
/SAPAPO/BOP - Backorder Processing in the
Background
/SAPAPO/AC03 - Product Availability
/SAPAPO/AC42 - Product Allocations

/SAPAPO/CDPSB0 - Production Planning Run
/SAPAPO/CDPSB1 - Production Planning Run in the
Background
/SAPAPO/RRP3 - Product View
/SAPAPO/RRP4 - Receipts View
/SAPAPO/RRP1 - Requirements View
/SAPAPO/PPT1 - Product Planning Table
/SAPAPO/PEG1 - Pegging Overview

/SAPAPO/VS01 - Interactive Vehicle Scheduling
/SAPAPO/VS05 - Schedule Optimization Run
/SAPAPO/VS551 - Release Shipments in the Background
/SAPAPO/VS531 - Delete Deliveries in the Background
/SAPAPO/VS541 - Delete Shipments in the Background

/SAPAPO/VERDELLD - Delete Planning Version
/SAPAPO/VERCOP - Copy Planning Version
/SAPAPO/MVM - Model and Version Management

/SAPAPO/LOC3 – Location
/SAPAPO/MAT1 – Product
/SAPAPO/RES01 – Resource
/SAPAPO/SCC_TL1 - Transportation Lane
S_AP9_75000130 - Maintain Means of Transport
/SAPAPO/TR_DELTRPR - Delete Transportation Lanes
/SAPAPO/SCC_TQ1 - Quota Arrangement
/SAPAPO/SCC03 - Production Process Model
/SAPAPO/CURTO_SIMU - Display Production Data
Structures

/SAPAPO/CC - CIF Cockpit
SMQ1 - qRFC Monitor (Outbound Queues)
SMQ2 - qRFC Monitor (Inbound Queues)
/SAPAPO/CQ - SCM Queue Manager

SE37 – ABAP Function Modules
SE38 – ABAP Editor
SE80 – ABAP Development Workbench
SM12 – Lock Entries
ST22 – Short Dump Analysis
SU01 - Users

/SCA/ICH – ICH
/SCA/ICH_S - ICH - Supplier View
/SCA/ICH_C - ICH - Customer View
/SCF/ICH_RR - Responsive Replenishment

OSS Notes Collection

APO in general:

370601 – Collective note: Performance in APO 3.0
303743 – Support Packages for APO Release 3.0A
438712 – Support Packages for APO Release 3.1
420669 – Collective Note: General Performance Improvement APO
420594 – Collective Note: Performance for DP 3.0A
447708 – Composite SAP note about APO system administration
500843 – Composite SAP note for COM and SAP liveCache >= 7.2

016083 – Standard jobs, reorganization jobs
195157 – Application log: Deletion of logs
375965 – APO Consulting: Alerts in Forecast
425825 – Consistency checks, /sapapo/om17, /sapapo/cif_deltareport
495166 – Tips and Tricks for Handling Alert Monitor
500063 – Overview of performance notes in Alert Monitor
519014 – Handling Planning Version Management
521639 – Generation of DP Alerts in Background
564186 – CLPSDP: Restriction in APO Collaborative Planning
572003 – SCM operating concept
830673 – AMON: Some consulting issues when handling alert monitor
844456 – AMON: Writing Alerts in background
877850 – Memory consumption / inconsistencies in liveCache
884334 – Alert Monitor: performance during alert determination

SAP BW and the database underlying SAP APO:

124532 – Performance when loading into BW

115407 – Loading large amounts if data
129252 – Oracle DB Statistics for BW tables
130253 – Notes on upload of transaction data into BW
130645 – Collective note: Performance SAP BW
130691 – Collective note for BW – tips and tricks
180605 – Oracle database parameter settings for BW
184905 – Collective note Performance BW 2.0
323090 – Performance problems due to degenerated indexes
325839 – Considerable increase of tablespace PSAPODSD
378509 – Oracle DP parameter setting for APO
384023 – Optimizing performance for ODS object
400191 – Further processing of data from PSA
409641 – Examples of packet size dependency on ROIDOCPRMS
421795 – SAP_ANALYZE_ALL_INFOCUBES report
428212 – Update of statistics of InfoCubes with BRCONNECT
458077 – For all entries: Performance problems in APO Demand Planning
459188 – Many small partitions in PSA tables under Oracle
485878 – DB2/390: BW: Partitioning the PSA tables
535986 – Monitoring for BW fact tables under Oracle
558563 – How does the client copy work with Demand Planning?

APO global Available to Promise (gATP) module

609435 – Composite SAP note: Performance Backorder Processing
610704 – Composite SAP note: Performance of SD documents update in APO

501446 – List of all Composite SAP notes for APO ATP
503158 – Allocations: Composite SAP note (3.0A, 3.1)
501880 – Allocations: Composite SAP note to connect DP (3.0A, 3.1)
382746 – Shipment and transportation scheduling with APO
383648 – Shipment scheduling as of APO 3.0A: Consulting notes

375193 – Backorder processing: Composite SAP note updating
389618 – APO initial supply with sales orders
873689 – Collective note for gATP performance in SCM 5.0
806562 – Collective note for gATP performance in SCM 4.1
650449 – Collective note for gATP performance in SCM 4.0
420598 – Composite SAP note for gATP performance in APO 3.1
420605 – Composite SAP note for gATP performance in APO 3.0A

APO Demand Planning (DP) module

897887 – Performance improvement in life cycle planning
892940 – MC62 and generation of CVC's: performance improvement
880012 – Macros: performance improvements
848109 - /SAPAPO/TS_PAREA_DE_INITIALIZE: Performance
832393 – Release Restrictions for SCM 5.0
394076 – Consulting: USER-EXITS and BAdIs in the forecast
350065 – Consultation: user parameters in forecast
200347 – Demand Planning: How does lock logic work? (2.0A)
301488 – Demand Planning: Actions after 3.0A upgrade
333243 – Analysis for faulty definition and execution of macros
350381 – Promotion: report for updating active promotions
354660 – Advice APO 3.0/3.1 life cycle planning
359761 – Demand Planning: loading performance data
360935 – Demand Planning 3.0: Realignment tool – consulting
363092 – Demand Planning: Performance Mass Processing
363221 – Consulting: Proportional factors / version copy
366650 – APO 3.0 promotion: update promotions w/ check of consistency
367031 – Update advice promotion: /SAPAPO/PROMOTION_UPDATE_30
373756 – Data extraction from Planning Area
374681 – Selections in mass processing
384550 – APO 3.0 promotion: Consulting: Reporting
388216 – Collective note consulting forecast
388260 – APO Consulting forecast: Automatic model selection
391625 – Backup and Recover for APO 3.0A Demand Planning

393655 – DP 3.0: administer performance
397292 – DP 3.0: How does the lock logic work?
398726 – DP 3.0: Performance Planning Book / Data View
402046 – DP 3.0: "No liveCache anchor found"
403050 – Consulting DP 3.0: Release from DP to SNP
412429 – Definition of jobs with macros
413525 – Consultation: Navigation attributes versus basic characteristics
420927 – Data extraction of selected key figures
425825 – Consistency checks, /SAPAPOOM17, /SAPAPO/CIF_DELTAREPORT
426806 – Memory/performance problems during extraction
428102 – Performance: Loading Planning Area Version
454644 – Consultancy: Lock Logic in Promotion Planning
482494 – Loading data from liveCache: Performance optimization
488020 – Performance improvement of the detailed proportion calculation
492399 – Realignment Tool: consulting
492460 – Check double entries in Planning Object Structure
495027 – Changing delivered APO InfoObjects (9A*)
503363 – Use & management of fixed aggregates in Demand Planning
505886 – Performance improvement during drilldown
506393 – Conversion exits when creating characteristic combinations
509479 – Elimination of inconsistencies in time series objects
510639 – Assignment of aggregates of Planning Object Structures
512184 – Background processing: Periodically delete job log
514593 – Performance improvement with DP background Processing
514971 – SAP Library documentation release 3.0 and 3.1 for DP
515120 – Performance of extraction of InfoCube-based key figures
515523 – Unexpected numerical results in Demand Planning
520876 – Inconsistencies in time series objects
529663 – Performance during /SAPAPO/TS_LCM_CONS_CHECK

541946 – Error message time series/period pattern does not exist

549184 – FAQ: What is important for extraction?

558563 – How does a client copy work with Demand Planning?

558995 – Advice on consistency report for forecast profiles

566527 – Composite SAP note for Demand Planning performance in APO 3.1

568671 – Collective consulting note on versions

568669 – Collective consulting note on release DP – SNP

570397 – Consulting: Workaround – Copying Planning Object Structures

571629 – How does the note management work?

573127 – Creating several characteristic combinations: /SAPAPO/MC62

576015 – Collective consulting note for Demand Planning

APO Supply Network Planning (SNP) module

572579 – Deletion of Location Master

571031 - Handling deletion of Product master or location product

771643 - Display MTO production and/or forecast without final assembly

155015 - SNP: Calender of resources and timestreams

827549 - Storage resources and the capacity view

838354 - Capacity variants of resources in SNP (APO 3.x)

727719 - Capacity variants of resources in SNP

722706 - SNP: Calculation of resource consumption of stock transfers

550330 - Consulting note about APO resources

674838 - Resource transfer from APO Release 4.0

516260 – PPM generation: Functionality description (II)

323884 – PPM Conversion: Description PPM conv. PP/DS -> SNP

494486 – PPM: Bucket consumption calculation during generation

525433 – PPM generation with lot size margin: consumption det.

455265 - PPM generation: new user exit

771279 - Assigning the R/3 production version with SNP planned orders
709884 - Consulting notes for PDS and ERP-PDS
525433 - PPM generation with lot size margin: consumption det.
568933 - External procurement relationship costs and currency
582212 - External planning (Documentation)
601990 - External relationships (documentation)
392712 - SPN orders in the PP/DS detailed planning
481906 - SNP - PP/DS integration (documentation)
519014 – Handling Planning Version Mgmt
568671 - Collective consulting note on versions
737230 - Consulting: Planning in technical periods
374375 - Use of time-dependent target days' supply
378229 - Time dependent target days supply in SNP
453644 - No use of navigation attributes in SNP
631351 - Add key figure details to a planning area
374375 - Use of time-dependent target days' supply
654235 - Using net change planning in SNP heuristic
574321 - SNP does not support any shelf life
503109 - Periodic Lot Sizes in the SNP Heuristic
626553 - Capacity leveling: Backward/forward scheduling
685780 - Capacity leveling: Scheduling orders
679233 - Capacity leveling: Planning split input help deletes entries
676281 - Capacity leveling: Adhering to minimum lot size
670893 - PPM validity ends within the bucket
650232 - Capacity leveling: Planning situation remains unchanged
623374 - Capacity leveling: Selection profile not taken into account
620059 - Capacity leveling: Orders are not deleted in OLTP
579556 - Taking shelf life into account with SNP optimizer
485018 - Info on the Performance of the Optimizer
703361 - Safety days' supply and SNP optimizer
810198 - SNP optimizer: Transportation costs

587407 - Optimization-Based Planning in SNP: The System Steps (attachment)
732698 - Interchangeability and SNP optimization
544877 - Storage cost handling
448986 - Information about Optimizer Lot Sizes
713590 - Calculating quotas in Linear Program
503222 - Info on Optimizer Production Order Splitting
379006 - Transport duration and planned delivery time in APO and R/3
420648 - Scheduling of stock transfers and VMI orders
361308 - Stock transf. releases: Scheduling via plnd. dely. time
441622 - Supplying-plant-dependent planned del. time/trans. Time
333386 - Availability date different in APO and R/3
617567 - Prerequisites for the extended safety stock planning
855592 - Dynamic safety stock in the PP/DS planning
557676 - Dynamic safety stock in PP/DS planning
646738 - SNP standard planning book for safety stock planning
862251 - Interactive SNP: 'Safety stock (planned)'
504253 - SNP: Standard Methods of Safety Stock Planning
644485 - Time-based disaggregation of safety stock values
617567 - Prerequisites for the extended safety stock planning
547049 - Cycle detection with the safety stock planning
602067 - Interpreting negative safety stocks
830673 - AMON: Some consulting issues when handling alert monitor
416489 - Resource alerts cannot be generated
481707 - SNP deployment / optimizer planning horizon
701438 - Deployment Optimizer ignores reqmts. ATD quantities
812709 - Composite SAP note: Performance of SNP in SCM 4.1
753137 - Composite SAP note: Performance in SNP for SCM 4.0
644676 - Consulting note on RLCDELETE report
586948 - VMI process: Recommendations and restrictions
724680 - Create SNP planned orders during transfer from R/3 to APO
699104 - Start SNP interactive planning with authorization concept
507810 - BW Reporting with SNP RemoteCubes
414965 - Release DP/SNP: Requirements also on non-workdays
568669 - Collective consulting note on release DP - SNP

702377 - /SAPAPO/OM_REORG_DAILY report deletes forecast
684946 - Release of constrained forecasts from SNP to DP
196773 - Warehouse stocks in interactive planning SNP

APO Production Planning/Detailed Scheduling (PP/DS) module

4267-5 – Guidelines for note searching in APO-PPS
370601 – Composite SAP Note: APO 3.0 and 3.1 performance
420669 – Collective note: General Performance Improvement APO
134164 – Optimizer RFC connection error
143314 – APO-R/3 Integration in Production Planning
195157 – Application log: deletion of logs
307336 – Object locked by user
331664 – APO PP/DS: material status
358833 – APO planned order conversion: check on material status
362208 – Creating de-allocated orders in APO
379567 – Performance: creating the detailed scheduling planning board
385602 – Validity in APO (Documentation)
390850 – Scrap in APO and R/3 (Documentation)
393437 – Pegging in APO: Background information
393634 – Release of the optimization server after terminations
394113 – Date shift between R/3 and APO
394184 – No subsequent processes after liveCache initialization
397989 – PP/DS: Scheduling (Documentation)
417461 – Scheduling error transferring orders to APO
426563 – CTP: Setting, system behavior and performance (Documentation)
431171 – Quota heuristic: planning of shortage/excess quantities
435130 – APO 3.1: Importing on optimizer version
435366 – BadI for additional checks when converting orders
439596 – Notes on customizing planning processes
441102 – Consulting notes in PP/DS
441740 – Planning time fence in APO (Documentation)

445899 – Problems in planning with sequence-dependent setup times

448960 – Net requirements calculation (Documentation)

449565 – Integration with CDP in APO (characteristics dependent planning)

457657 – Search function for planning orders in application log

457723 – Planning period with PP heuristics

458996 – Fixed pegging in SAP APO (Documentation)

459694 – Finite scheduling with CTP or SAP_MRP_002 (Documentation)

460107 – Fallback strategy to avoid scheduling errors

481906 – SNP-PP/DS integration (Documentation)

513827 – Settings/parallel processing in the PP/DP planning

517264 – Documentation: Master Data functions in APO

518556 – Using heuristics in the production planning run

519070 – Planning without final assembly

520561 – Maintaining product master in R/3 or in APO?

525571 – MOP: Function restrictions

528913 – Lock R/3 data transfer during SNP, CTM. PP/DS planning

532979 – Pegging in optimization

550330 – Consulting note about APO resources

557731 – Planning file entry + reuse mode (Documentation)

560683 – Resource selection for PP/DS optimization

560969 – Rescheduling: Bottom-up (SAP_PP_009_

572996 – Simultaneously started optimization runs

575624 – Locking concept in APO PP/DS (Documentation)

577158 – Withdrawal from alternative plant in APO (Documentation)

578044 – Additional parameters for optimization

579758 – R/3 → APO: Retaining APO scheduling activity dates

582212 – External planning (Documentation)

584204 – Planning standard lots for continuous I/O (SAP_PP_C001)

591115 – MRP areas in APO (Documentation)

603828 – APO 4.0: Importing and optimizer version

605855 – Enqueue queue time in the syslog for parallel MRP

606320 – R/3 data transfer during PP/DS optimization run

606334 – Overlap of activities after PP/DS optimization run

607428 – Product planning table – FAQ's

615877 – Integration/delta report manufacturing orders: performance

619976 – Special procurement types in APO (Documentation)

627377 – Consulting Note: Model-Mix-Planning and Sequencing

630565 – Guidelines for SAPNet – R/3 Front-end notes in PP/DS Optimizer

644676 – Consulting note on RLCDELETE report

654312 – Release restriction for SCM 4.0

660113 – Performance: setting up DS planning board for Release 4.0

660194 – RLCDELETE does not delete the selected orders

660857 – MOP FAQ's: Answers to frequently asked question about MOP

664022 – Setting of performance functions

679118 – Which operations are performed by /SAPAPO/OM_REORG_DAILY?

681656 – Objective function in PP/DS optimization

689101 – PP/DS optimization consulting

690887 – Deletion report: no list display of undeleted orders

698417 – Fixed pegging: supported document flows and document changes

703774 – SCM 4.1: Importing and APO Optimizer version

704583 – Fixed pegging in APO: symptoms and restrictions

707184 – Documentation: Functions of master data in APO 4.0

709884 – Consulting notes for PDS and ERP-PDS

711235 – Project Manufacturing with SCM 4.1: Collective Note

712066 – Restrictions of the PP/DS Optimizer

766827 – Composite SAP note: Performance SCM 4.0

778261 – Prerequisites for secondary resources

808671 – PP: liveCache alerts out of the given validity are displayed

834838 – Planning board: No dialog box for performance warning

879324 – Composite SAP Note for PP/DS performance in SCM APO 4.0

879531 – Composite SAP Note for PP/DS performance in SCM APO 4.1

APO Transportation Planning/Vehicle Scheduling (TP/VS) module

514897 – Collective note: Performance TPVS (only valid for APO 3.x)

303743 – Support Packages for APO Release 3.0A

436687 – Collective Note: Performance APO Integration

439438 – Collective Note: Performance APO Delta Report

392302 – Collective note for Transportation Planning

362445 – Effect of doc. changes in R/3 on APO shipments

566319 – Composite SAP consulting note APO TP/VS

439577 – Data selection using location in the TP/VS

529813 – Performance in TP/VS shipment handling

448487 – Transportation planning: Integration of R/3 and APO

628476 – Resource selection in /SAPAPO/vs01

730774 – Selection or Sales Orders by target location (only valid for 3.x)

604789 – Performance of the TP/VS "Inbound Controller"

624619 – Implementing user filtering of orders in TP/VS (only valid for 4.0)